WRITING THE TIDES

Writing the Tides

NEW AND SELECTED POEMS

KEVIN ROBERTS

RONSDALE PRESS

WRITING THE TIDES
Copyright © 2006 Kevin Roberts

RONSDALE PRESS
3350 West 21st Avenue
Vancouver, B.C., Canada V6S 1G7
www.ronsdalepress.com

Typesetting: Julie Cochrane, in New Baskerville 11 pt on 13.5
Cover Design: Julie Cochrane
Cover Photo: Julie Cochrane
Paper: Ancient Forest Friendly Rolland "Enviro" — 100% post-consumer
    waste, totally chlorine-free and acid-free

Ronsdale Press wishes to thank the Canada Council for the Arts, the Government of Canada through the Book Publishing Industry Development Program (BPIDP), and the Province of British Columbia through the British Columbia Arts Council for their support of its publishing program.

Library and Archives Canada Cataloguing in Publication

Roberts, Kevin, 1940–
    Writing the tides: new and selected poems / Kevin Roberts.

Includes one poem translated into Chinese.
ISBN-13: 978-1-55380-036-1
ISBN-10: 1-55380-036-2

    I. Title.

PS8585.O297W75 2006   C811'.54   C2006-900421-8

At Ronsdale Press we are committed to protecting the environment. To this end we are working with Markets Initiative (www.oldgrowthfree.com) and printers to phase out our use of paper produced from ancient forests. This book is one step towards that goal.

Printed in Canada by Marquis Printing, Quebec

CONTENTS

ACKNOWLEDGEMENTS

A number of the new poems in this collection were first published in the *Malahat Review, Descant, Canadian Literature, Friendly St. Reader* and *The Australian*. Harbour Publishing, Oolichan Books, Wakefield Press, Beau Geste Press and Ronsdale Press were responsible for publication of the earlier collections. CBC Radio broadcast both *S'Ney'Mos* and *Stonefish*. My thanks to Ralph Maud, Roger Allan, Ronald Hatch and George Amabile for their patience, insight and assistance. A special thanks goes out to my wife, Maria, who sat with me while we made the final choice of poems — those that went into the collection and those that were consigned to limbo.

Writing the Tides

Safe on the sea anchor
parachute like a huge dahlia
blooming below the sea's face
cursed to ride our short voyage
in flow and ebb, ebb and flow
time to scribble nautical notes
plumb line depth and sound
the winding current, dead reckon
the destination and the reason
for the voyage

clever hands have carved the keel
stem and stern and bow
rough hewn rudder, sewn sails
ribs and lapstrake, caulk
and copper bottom
floated an iron needle
in the haystack world
to con us true north

yet this map arterial
is merely the brain's terrain
consoles the eyes' stub
on the tangle of stars
the stumble step need
for any, some, one,
true blue direction

and underneath, the tide maddens us
with fluidity, silver trickle growing
to dark flood at the moon's whim
our desire too, moves lunar and lunatic
under the blue-veined orb
so brief, oh brief
the breath and scrabble
in the unscripted play
we speak in our puny way
of "a tide in the affairs of men"
pretentious puff fish out of
any true element and master of none

and still we scratch these signs
uncertain, guessing wild
at the longitude
and latitude of flesh
riding only certainly
on the ebb and flow
the flow and ebb
of the tides.

from
CARIBOO FISHING
NOTES

In February we augured
two two-foot holes   the lake frozen
three-feet deep our woollen mittens
chunky as cast iron with icicles
from clearing out the holes
as we dug down

and we jacked off the short rods
for an hour   jaw bones
electric with cold
sitting on camp stools
tossing Jolly Green Giant corn
down the black holes   crouched
staring into ourselves
while the wind crawled
coldly over our kidneys

and an old Greek walked
out over the frozen water to see us
offered us hot buttered rum
from a hip flask the left arm
of his red-check lumber jacket
empty   pinned neatly to his side

In early May big rainbows came on
in Dragon Lake   Kamloops trout
crazy for hatching shrimp oozing up
from the reeds of the middle islands
and we clobbered them with something red
teal and red   trolled   drifted Royal Coachman
and hungry for *mana* a tiny fluorescent
flatfish on a split cane rod

and I played one four-pounder west of the first island
till my wrist was soft as butter
my will almost gone

it was my partner who struck so hard
pulled the treble hook
clean out of the flatfish

sitting cramped in the drifting boat
ice still on in the shade
eyes bright
for the quick slash of the rod's tip
oiled spurt of the reel

Jack O'Spades on the bends
in the snow ruts before Wells
the ice off creek's entrance
deep aquamarine
and five-pound Dolly Varden struck
in slackbellied rushes from
under the ice
starved and thin
the pink flesh tore like
wet newspaper
as we opened shrunken gut

You have to hand it to
rainbow trout

tricked and hooked
they die like ballet dancers
leap and turn
sinuous as oil
graceful as clouds

choreography by Pan

I could not do it
that way

In the end I chose
not to fish the streams
white water caught boiling away
to its own thin conclusions

the lakes finally held me
narcissistic   ovoid
drew me deeper into
their dark flesh

Physica the old Greek said
smacking the cedar beams with one arm
in his shack near Ten Mile Lake
sipping ouzo and water
pulling a match flame off his boot
you got to do it natural the smoke
wandering up around eyebrows
thick as your finger

still fish   he cried
bloody water's too dangerous
to go roaring about

throwing open his freezer chest
white and silver with trout

no rush just
wait for the buggers

but we did not

thinking of deep green shadows
shimmering always
at the other end
of the reeds

Late May and the word came from
McLeese Lake haunted by emerald
shadows of restless rainbows

and we came steaming down the Cariboo
Highway at 3 a.m. curving with the Fraser
River   morning ice whisking into spray off
the '53 Chev's bonnet shuddering to Eaton's
snow tyre retreads on the back
the driver's door epileptic at fifty
nylon rope fraying
on the roof rack
chanting in the wind

met them at dawn with black gnat and
sinking line
lured them into a hole by the picnic grounds
taking seven silver one-pounders
bright as a dime
by the time the lace of mist
unspun itself in the sun

at nine o'clock we gave it up   came
wobbling like a Meps spinner to Quesnel
the Chev yawing against the wind under the boat
and at Australian the action was so bad
I got the mechanic to hoist the car
while we slit the trout outside
and the steering pin fell out in two

fell straight out into that grease black hand

two thick rusty bits of steel worn through
an inch long each
sharpened bright as a chisel edge with wear
shiny as a Deadly Dick

and he juggled them like dice in that
oil-grained hand
grinning at our silence

I could not answer him
when he asked
how many fish
we had caught

June and a lace mist
climbing a logging track
out of Horsefly and a
lake
rose suddenly out of the mountains
had no name
we could find

firs stood
arms linked against us
a dark place the water
black with
many inlets

serrations in the coin
of our understanding

and when we did hook
rainbows it was as if
the lake turned away
casually flicked them up at us
to see our backs

cleaned and fried them with two
strips of bacon
smoke greasing the mist the
pink white flesh peeled
off the bone
casual as thought

The late summer sun
burned the water to soup
sent the trout deep and
we could trick them
only at sunset on Ten Mile
with Royal Coachman flicked dry
near the edge of the reeds
at lethargic swirls

and the old Greek sat hunched
over the navel of the lake
anchored tight
bobbing in the water-skiers' wakes
dark green punt ten-foot split cane rod
patiently plumbing the jaded
appetites of the trout

In late August everyone fished Ten Mile
for Oregon rainbows big and tough

alders spat broken orange and yellow
teeth all over the water firs
bowed together in dark conceits

but a line tangled
in the six-horse Merc prop
coughing burnt oil
balled   choked and twisted in a knot

in the late evening it was simpler
J.W. and I trolling a green nymph
no lead   in a wide figure eight

but I lost a big one when he jumped
and ran close in at the sight
of the white boat in the gloom
and my Mitchell reel jammed around the bar

and the old man with one arm
laughed when he saw it
sitting in the waist of Ten Mile Lake
green wooden punt anchored with
paint tin full of concrete
still fished with worms
staring at the mountains
sipping Kelowna Red against the chill

The last time we fished Ten Mile
it snowed as I pulled the one
seven-pound Oregon rainbow over the net
blunt snout limp tail and primitive eyes

we loaded the boat in big soft flakes
pulling on a bottle of Captain Morgan rum

it was the warden who told us
sitting in the Billy Barker
the old Greek died out there and no one
noticed for a couple of days
the ten-foot rod frozen into his body
hunched over an empty flagon of Kelowna Red

and when they pulled him and his punt
in to the shore
at dusk on the third day
a big rainbow trout was still hooked
swimming in endless circles
on his line

from
WEST COUNTRY

The Reach

And if the body does not
aspire
what then can I name

this looking out
through my eyes
at the blue burn sky
ripped by cloud

the woodpecker drum
echo on the roof
touch of wild fur
scent of burning cedar

again the path fills bitter
with ice

mountain above patched
and spiked with snow

like goats we pick our way up
in each other's footsteps

crows in stark alders stare
fluff up into black balls

what does the body
reach for?

learning the necessary dance
I forget the inevitable slip
and fall

does it come down to this
again?
what does the body
reach for?

at night the clear bark
of sea lions turning
in the cold sea

and the back log breaks
into two red flares

I turn to you
to your body warm in the dark

discover the body
reaches for itself

it reaches for
itself

Pas de Deux

in darkness

we celebrate
light

white arms

Icarus

stir of feathers
out &
around

wind lifts
a flutter of white
against
dark

again arms &
the slow
leap
out of the deep
well of flesh &
white radiance

cracks
into
man & woman
again against
dark
this song a reach
for the sun's
limbs

dance a white
swirl
turns into the hands
of many
lovers

consider the wings
white butterflies
rising

multitudes fluttering
to whiten
the dark

Skating down Trout

for Pat Lane

In winter on Lac la Hache
when cold snaps its fingers
quick
Indians skate down trout
over ice set two feet clear
till they scare up a big char
working it slowly
like sheep dogs
driving the dark-backed silver
glimmer closer into shore
turning back its runs
into deep water
the fish circling tighter
not knowing the shield
ice makes between
terror and shadows
impotent to touch it
in its element the trout
safe against all
but its own fears
forcing it shallower
closer to the clean cut skirr
of the skates
driven by forms
only the fish makes substance
until in panic
at the hiss and whir
of the steel blades it runs
defeats itself
char jammed trembling

between the gravel bottom
and the frozen ice
beating delicate fins
till axe blows
open up the ice
deliver the fish
to its hunters

hanging limp by the gills
in triumphant
thumb and finger

For Florence Morris

my brothers swore
she was the only woman
they wanted to marry

even that she took
with a wry smile
standing
in the disarray of her fortunes
with an ivory cameo
at her throat
an MBE & OBE fading inside
little plush cases

her husband
staring out from his photo
in mayoralty robes
in disbelief
at the tiny room jammed
with an oak piano with
brass candelabra & yellow keys
no one could play
left over from the estate
she sold block by block
till even the big house
went & unabashed she
poured tea in a Northfield
Housing Trust home
from a silver pot
kept the dog & her son
until they were both blind
& laughed with them both
at the world none of them saw
with much interest but

never missed a party
or a spot of sherry &
played bridge the night
she died
cheating
only her usual amount &
caught the last bus home
with the drunks

my brothers
carrying her coffin
past the stone named for her
outside the Congregational
church in Highgate
swear they heard her
chuckling
when they stumbled
down the steps

Heritage

for J.D.R.

one was Cornish to his miner's boots
and Broken Hill cough
great hands like leather
holding the Methodist Hymn Book
singing with the pain of a wild Celt

the other was a burgher who loved
company   good Scotch   horses
and beautiful women

one slugged out a life of sorts
at Moonta pit face unwrapped wax paper
around a lunch of Cornish pastie & strong
black tea
sang "Solidarity Forever" with conviction
enjoying the music even more
sent his thick limbed sons out to work at twelve

the other hung up his Light Horse sabre after Egypt
turned his charm into money
presided at Mayoralty luncheons of grilled
whiting washed down with a good Reynella white
saw his name carved in foundation stones
at Unley Oval and Gardens opposite
endowed the Highgate Church
and the Home for the Incurables
met the Queen once
built a great house at Myrtle Bank out of
Mt. Gambier stone and invited promising
young men for tennis or to meet his daughters

refused to recognize the advent
of the horseless carriage
and died just before it ruined him

one sat in the other's Gardens
until his face gnarled under his flat
cloth cap to match the walking stick
he rested both heavy hands upon
listening to concerts the other began
but was too busy to attend

the marriage was gossiped about
either well beneath or
far too above

in the other country
they would never have met

To Know the Medium

is to know
the garden is not lost it
blooms
about us
it is eyes that
cannot speak like
"fish
who cannot see
water" or
Lear complete only in a storm or
termites building blind
two footings
the two bends
of the eyeless faith
reaching to complete
the arch

or my brother Malcolm & I
at Fisherman's Bay putting out
jam jars baited with bread
tiny whiting
drawn by the tide
butting against glass
as we splashed towards them
held them up silver
in the stumbling sun

or today the hummingbirds
blood red whirr to feed
insistent upon sweetness

and my brother gone down
to some luxuriant
misplaced flower
in his guts

and the going down   what of that move
to earth
and with it in the same
gesture this garden
which binds them all
blind always
binds me to this

Ghazal

rain the grain flung from
the bent fingers of the wind

only the smell of love keeps me here
death tongue-tied dances in its green plastic bag

Look. The indelible colour of the universe
washes off on my hands

my heart beats rock'n'roll against my classic breath
run with my twin Anubis

tongues over bare teeth
kiss me now, damn you, Miss Death!

though I have cut and pruned the apple tree
it grows its holes back to the sky

Spanish Banks

this morning the beach
is a desert
no explorer loved
sand grimaces   seagulls
retch overhead   logs huddle
like old drunks on the tide-line

in the necklace the tide wove
all the lost things gather
broken shells   half-buried boxes
plastic bags   rusted wire rope
bald-headed kelp

I trace last night's tracks
above the line the tide dissolves
two   tentative
exploring each other
merge of scuffed sand
hear again laughter
from a tossed head

tracks run   stop
face each other
backtracking   the other time
rises like a forty-foot swell

there were words then
but your eyes
broke the silence

your fingers ran along my lips
but the way you looked
through me

I turned quickly   convinced
someone was standing
behind us

Brighton Beach

surf rattles its knuckles
on the shore
shingle makes tiny gossip
skittering and popping

greater mortality lies
in the tightness of your lower lip
flare of your black greatcoat
as you pace the beach

we are waiting to say it to each other

something sits on us spindly legged
rusty as the whorls
and blistered silver coronets
wrought long ago on Palace Pier

your hair tied back so hard
your forehead shines with the need
to lay it on the table
smooth your fingers through
the rough cloth of our love

but we don't in this place
of Imperial rust
that crystallizes change
without changing
knowing it would sound as hollow
and exotic as Brighton Palace
and we are not an Empire or an Age
leaving colonels in bath chairs
stiffening in the cold sun
on the promenade

like this sea and sand and tide
we move in and out
of each other's reach
grating in love one upon the other

incompatible finally
though resting totally
in each other's grip

Frantoto Ikaria

here the wind
forms no lips
blows no tune
dry grass weaves as one fear
ripples a startled sheep wave
along stark mountain terraces

the soil shards and pebbles
family plots clutching rock walls
worked hand and back and thigh

kneeling to scythe grass for winter hay
men grow into granite
women's bodies
to the rhythmic sob of the hoe
sink thicker into hips of earth

olive trees scarify
figs sacrifice leaves for juice
behind granite outcrops
in tiny valleys of trickling springs
vines struggle into grapes

sparse stone houses
stones on slate roofs against the wind
stone on stone fitted long ago
built behind ridges   in hollows
hidden from Arab raiders three deaths ago
standing out to sea off Evdilos
rocking softly in dhows
hands on knives
watching for tell-tale lights
a betrayal of candles

only the church faithful
multiplying maggot-white bell towers
lemon-eyed Christs gilt framed
hangings of brocaded silk
and hived in them the black priests
sting of sin billowing in their black soutanes
soft lipped   lush bearded
white hands render the villagers to Caesar
white hands lighting candles at gilt altars
white hands

turning to bless

For Maria

my Ikarian beauty
olive is our love

wings on your smile
but never the sun

Aubade: Exeter

the blackbird is in the garden

glissando   notes like a fast
run tape   staple the silence

the fist of night
opens on a pearl
glowing about my lids

my hands fill with the soft
weight of your breasts

you sleep like the messenger from Marathon
run open-mouthed into the earth

I pull a strand of hair
wet black for the corner of your lips

a tiny pulse struggles like a worm
in the skin over your eye

we have always been like this
curled in soft mother-of-pearl
together

two milk bottles   two
ringing chunks on the front step
the slight limp taps-ta-taps
down the path

somewhere another bird is trilling

I grab the telephone
at the third ring

no one answers

it keeps me wide awake
in the grey dawn

Trans-Canada

for Dale Lovick

east and west the highway runs
across migration lines

everyone drives it
trucks semis buses cars
remark its flat face roll by
coulees and wild grass   full
to the wide circle horizon

out of Portage la Prairie
and every mile some life
fails the North South
natural crossing
road kill
crushed by the trucks

clump of feather
spattered flesh

near Moose Jaw
a bit of fur
ripples in the wind
pasted to this inexorable line

crows and hawks
on telephone lines
by Medicine Hat
waiting

in the Kamloops Hotel
the lead guitarist hot
at triple timing
but no one is listening

drinking Labatts beer
Old Dutch potato chips
beef jerky and pickled eggs
watching the Canucks losing
to the Canadiens on CBC
Hockey Night in Canada

but I kept seeing that deer
crumpled by the Eaton's truck
legs still jerking as the casual beaks
dropped in

and in the hotel washroom mirror
I saw my body built
against the seasons

on this line

a mere pelt
flung in trade
upon the prairies

from

S'NEY'MOS

a small white-washed tower
on Front Street
fir logs three feet thick
hand cut
adzed and fitted by eye
firing slits
all around
impenetrable in those times

1858 and the townspeople
of S'ney'mos
straining to hear the Manager
in mutton chops on tiptoe
moleskin trousers, striped work
shirts
flyaway coats, bonnets
bobbing and a child squalling
and squalling and the rumour
of an Indian raid and the child
hushed
and wide-eyed
and hushed

climbing the circular stairs
to the second floor lookout
in the light of narrow
chinks
slits
cut for rifles and cannon
that fired grapeshot and
chainshot
at Protection Island opposite
smashing a jagged rent
a smoking scar through the trees
a warning to

Haida Indians sitting offshore
in war canoes
hushed
by the severed firs' mangled boughs
stunned by the voice that
shouted such hate
turned out of S'ney'mos harbour
paddled North again

࿊

S'ney'mos
the place of the stream
where the wolves
lost their fur   began
to speak naked
together

it is not a
meeting of people

this running of tides
against a certain
spot
on earth

it is the ninth wave
& wake of the
S.S. *Beaver*
over the unsuspecting
canoe

washes it high
to hang
under a roof
on Commercial Street

the second floor contains
cutlasses snuff-boxes letters
yellowing into authority
powder flasks & photos of men
fierce eyes
thumbing waistcoats

and the good burgher's wife's
best plate
the rose set they dined on
salmon grouse venison
& rosehip wine
after hanging the first man
in Nanaimo
an Indian
whose pursuit
named a river
whose death on the yard arm
of the Hudson's Bay frigate
named Gallows Point
shrivelled the hearts
of his family
silent on the shore

January and frost
still
white on the earth

∞

the land sighs
a great crush
of earth
upon trees leaves ferns

beyond imagination
this growing
deep
under the soil

shine and gloss
facet of this
fruit

consider the short
breath of man
walking deep
into this event

pitlamps & steel
drills
to pick
these black
apples of coal

∞

Dunsmuir the bully boy
on his porch
in a morning suit
and vest
pulls out his god
Hunter to check
the starting whistle
for second shift No. 1

takes his tea
in a porcelain cup
from his fluttering
aide says
seventeen sick again today?
malingerers   we must
hire more Chinese
they take the work
better

under S'ney'mos harbour
mine tunnels
honeycomb deep
earth

props of coal ships
rumble
overhead

gas seep
pulls itself
into a gasp
flash

explosion running
like wild surf

along the face
rippling
like a belly punch

and these died slowly
lungs bubbling
black froth

> *some calling upon the Lord*
> *some upon their wives &*
> *children poorly left*
> *some blaspheming till the end*

one climbing on top
of the living
pushing their heads
under
nails
clawing at the mine
face.

Who knows what hands
carved his bloated valediction
on a headstone leaning
sideways in a park

> Joseph Mairs, 21 UMWA
> A Faithful Union Lad
> A Martyr to a Noble Cause
> The Emancipation of his Fellow Man

thrown by the careless
hip of history
his stone now holds
small ground
his flesh long gone
under a city
throbbing beyond his ken.

> In Memory of
> Michael Corcoran
> Native of Kerry, Ireland
> Killed in the explosion
> May 3, 1887

A Perrenna Ricordanza
Della Infausta Explosione
Belloni Giovanni
Nativo di Venezia
May 3, 1887

On mudflats
south of Nanaimo
an Indian shack
gutted

roof peaks fired
to a black
gloss
above a hollow
shell

through the charred
door frame
flame has feathered
wood

a double bed
sags
under an invisible
weight

coils
collapsed in soft
twists
of wire

what was consummated here
fire alone knows

Li' Fire over K'un Earth

the struggle bringing no renewal
at this time

only grass grows higher
in praise of ash

Mah Fung

And these also
Among the dead
Chinamen nos. 7,
23 and 11,
names unknown
May 3, 1887

And Lee Kung leaned forward
With the papers
And his gold rings flashed
And he said
Is it not better to labour
for ten years
among the barbarians
and gain respect upon one's return
than to live and die in poverty
here in Kiang-Tze
and be a bare branch
unremembered by one's sons?

and Mah Fung looked at Mai Wong's bright eyes
and made his mark upon the papers

and was seasick for five weeks
on the voyage

and felt his stomach rise again
to his mouth
the first time they dropped him
faster than a stone
in the cage down No 1 Mine

and in the darkness
he swung his pick and wound
the gutbuster into the black coal face
dreaming of the green
terraced rice fields Lee Kung
was buying for him every month
a day's walk from the village
of Kiang-Tze and Mai Wong's
bright eyes   and as well
the gold piece he bought
at the Hudson's Bay Bank
every two months and buried
in the dirt floor of his shack

and the seasons merged
with the dark of the pit face
and Lee Kung's letter
he folded and unfolded
and read till it fell
in squares and he could no longer
read of the new law
that took his bright
terraced rice fields and his money
and of the marriage of Mai Wong

and he dug up twenty-four gold pieces
polished them and bought land
from the barbarians and grew vegetables
and sold them and buried more gold
pieces in his land at night and coughed
in the pit face and buried more gold pieces
until each Spring when he planted
cabbages and potatoes his spade
turned the old gold pieces in
with the bright new ones and the seeds

and he leaned on his shovel
to cough up the black dust
and saw the dark mountains
above him tipped with snow and dark
trees all about the edge of his field

and looked down one day after rain
and saw in a big pool of still water
that his beard and hair were white

and went that day to buy
ship passage back to Kiang-Tze
May 3, 1887, his last shift
in No. 1 mine and coughed so much
he was on his knees
when the first explosion burst
the pit face and buried him
squatting like an ancient foetus
in the middle of the earth.

死者中还有这些：

中国人 7 号，
23 号，和 11 号
姓名未知
1887 年 5 月 3 号

李康身体前倾，手中拿着契约
金戒指熠熠发光，说道
与其在江柘贫困潦倒一生
孑然一身
淡忘在
子孙的记忆里
不如在白鬼佬那里苦干十年
挣他个钵满盆满
然后
衣锦还乡荣归故里。

马枫注视着梅雯
明亮的双眸，灿烂的微笑
签字画押

漫漫海上航行
晕船五个礼拜

当第一次乘坐罐笼下到一号矿井
他感到
下落得比石头坠地还快
胃好像一下子升了起来
到了嗓子眼

在黑暗中对着闪闪发亮的煤
使劲地抡着铁锹
旋转着风镐
梦想着

在距离江柘村一天行程的地方
李康每月为他购置
绿色的稻田
还有梅雯的微笑

每隔一个月
他还在哈得逊湾银行购买
金条
然后深埋于窝棚的地板之下

矿井作业面的黑暗消融了四季
李康的信
他读了一遍又一遍
折拢又展开，直至
裂成一方方碎片
他再也无法读到
新颁布的法律没收了他美丽的稻田
也无从了解他与梅雯的婚姻

他挖起二十四根金条
把它们擦得铮亮
从白鬼佬手中买来土地并种上庄稼
然后卖掉
趁着夜色在地头埋下更多的金条

又在矿面上咳嗽
埋藏更多的金条，

直到春暖花开
他种上大白菜，土豆，豆子
他用铁铲把原来的金条埋回原处
同时埋下新的金条
播下种子

他倚靠着铁铲
咳出黑乎乎的煤灰
周围的山阴沉沉的
顶上积着雪
田地的四周
围着黑压压的树木

一天雨后
他低下头
在水池中
看到
须发全白了

1887 年 5 月 3 日
他挖起很多的金条
当天就买了回江柘的船票
这是他在一号矿井的最后一班
他咳嗽得很厉害，人都跪下了
就在这时
第一次爆炸炸毁了矿面
埋葬了他

半蹲着，像远古的胎儿
留在了大地的深处。

– translation courtesy of Gary Jiang

from

STONEFISH

Stonefish

At age forty-two like a mink
he chewed his own foot
off
to save the pelt
caught in the stock exchange
leg trap

What did he see?
Gauguin limping about
the steamer
crags of Moorea sheer
volcanic thrust in the dawn
mist
ring of white
surf like a careless
necklace about the indolent
isle

the colour.   the colour.

from this moment his
eyes were alive
in this place where
all things curved
bright as vahines' hips

scent of frangipani
like wild incense

at first
his palette could not
contain it

that there are so many shades of blue
dusted to green & gold &
the light therein

it was their bodies
he painted
easy limbs
reclining
redolent
flowers red & white
at the hips   behind
the ears
women with shiny leaves
in their hair flowers about
their dark swan
necks
the great resting strength
of their bodies

꩜

Gauguin walks in thunder
rolling
so low the black
lava peaks
shake

rain like a tossed bucket
of water

and after
the sweet smell of
decay meets the frangipanis'
scent in mid air

that very moment
beauty so rich it turns

decadent   one joined
sense on this enchanted
isle
the colour of it
one booming truth
ringing
in Gauguin's ears

∞

And what cannot I
create?
Gauguin shouts above
the thunder his face wet
with warm rain

after all these things
Icarus, Jesus, Oviri

these small things
hang upon eyes

words I must turn to
colour
after the gold burn of
Vincent Van Gogh
my fire
alone

he eats his
paints
white first
down through the sun
to black his eyes
pushing the last
indulgence to
royal purple

Gauguin to Charles Morice

Tahiti, July 1901

I am a savage
a wolf in the woods
without a collar

Puvis will call a picture
Purity   and
to explain it
paint a young
virgin with a lily in her hand

Gauguin in *Purity* will paint
a landscape with a stream

no taint of civilized man

Puvis as a painter is a scholar
not a man of letters

Are the forms rudimentary?
they have to be!
Is the execution thereof
far too simple?
It has to be!

Emotions first!

Understanding later!

des fleurs!
toujours des fleurs!

in his paintings the strong
legs of vahines rise
like tap roots
from the coloured
earth

breasts   all
fruit

their bodies
quizzical at all this
fuss

passive
reclining
standing at rest

waiting

in *nevermore* for example
the light is green
gold thigh &
neck
black hair curled like a
snake

red slit
of a mouth
even the gold toes curl
belly at the height
of ripeness

waits for that precise
moment of release
the snake bite
into the apple
the involuntary lurch
into procreation

the Stonefish flare &
spit
of poison

under Gauguin's brush
her body grows like a rich
bruised fruit

Vert de Grèce

colour of bronze
figures
green with age

Gauguin searches
for an ancient copper
acetate/colour
a magic paint for
their bodies   himself
all the forms

finds the right
shade

the wise
decay of the Greek
Gods

⌾

who steps upon
the Stonefish

steps upon
his own image

atavistic

under the green
lagoon water

dark butterfly
out of
the soul's
cocoon

fluttering & distorted
by the waves

rock-like in the blue
green
water
the Stonefish hides
spines flared upon its
back

awaits the dancing
foot

∞

Gauguin does not tell
his wife
at night he takes
strong dark medicine

vahines
their brown thighs
flexing in his
hands he squeezes

the fruit pulps
like papaya sweet
to his touch

rots in his palms

in the morning he
sees the vivid colours
of his paints
dull by comparison

there is never
enough

light

Gauguin to Mette

July 1892

I have 50 francs in my
pocket
at this time &
do not know what to do

I have 32 canvasses
one of 3 metres by 1 metre 30
three of 1 metre or so by 90
and the remainder by 70

a fair number of drawings
and sketches

a few carved knick-knacks

I do not have
enough
to eat

      ∞

In Punamauia
the sins of his flesh
burst
out upon his body

he cannot reach up far
enough
for the fruit
breast
flower

the rich land
fails
to keep him
whole

guilt
grows sores
within his body

his Eve turns into
Oviri
animal/wolf
naked female death
spirit

consumes his flesh
with running guilt

sick red flowers
on his legs

he becomes his own
garden

the great Stonefish poison
syphilis
the white guilt

eruptions on his belly and
back

∞

Gauguin almost
believes
what he has made himself

Gauguin s'impose
la vie d'or l'âge
d'Eden
mais son âme est blessée
par tout le détritus
du Christ
dans ces îles

the Bishop preaches against him
keeps the village girls away
from the party in his hut

Gauguin carves Père Paillard
the bishop & a young Marquesan
girl copulating
in wood
on his front step

☙

Gauguin est mort
nous sommes tous perdus
Tioka the Marquesan cries &

Pastor Vernier sighs
in relief
happy at the triumph
of his Protestant God
over Oviri

the Bishop hurrying to Gauguin's
shack
to grab this
famous body
bury it in consecrated
ground

opens the shack
door
sees Gauguin's body still
warm
one leg dangling
from the bed

∞

Stonefish burrows content
into the white
sand

huddles its spines
flat

rests

from
DEEP LINE

Journey

to think
a journey
mapped sure
as this

salmon burning
cold silver

sea
shot with this
flame

you think they're
common
as gravel silt
ragged red clowns
in green
sick yellow
splotches
running pratfalls &
tumbles
upstream

wise as laughter

you wish for energy
built clear as this

maple-grained &
burning itself to
fine ash

you dream a journey
tracked certain
as this one

slowly years turn salmon
swim about strange meridians

consider you hands/face
fathom lines
deepening

you look for
colours of wisdom
in lovers &
others

in yourself.

Raincoast

sky
come down to
earth

water smoked and
curling
into sea

land
soaking
breathes in through
quiet skin

drops like soft
wet
cats paws

time is jelly fish
tendrils
trailing down
Desolation Sound

Easthope 7/9
muffling the rain
panting up the coast

mist turns into faces
of wistful girls

you run the lines out
dreaming

in this distance
nothing is
certain.

Off Lasqueti

for Thor Johnson

We clean fish
all day

200 coho
anonymous flesh
thumping into the hold
gulls and dogfish thrashing
astern for gills
like red dahlias
huge pink worms
of guts

blood seeps into
everything

scales
like mica fragments
on our faces
on our hands
as we eat

scrub the gutting box &
deck to break the slip
of the slime & black
dry blood

all this killing
grows
like scales over
my eyes

he says you got to
think of it
as a harvest

I dream of spoons
like scythes
threshing
in the deep.

52 Ways

for Peter Such

this man
struggles to tell you
turning a Tom Mack 4½
in his hand
of the magic of its
bright dimples
ties the right colour
hoochie for June with
his teeth and hands
waves an open palm
for the speed dip &
final flip of a
Blackfish Sound no 1

this man struggles
to tell you of
a hooker's love for
a good chokerman
arm a Madill spar &
keeping the road below
clear

this man struggles
to tell you
that in the end
the red bark peels
from an arbutus
reveals green trunk
split green
later
it will burn
bright as coal.

The Fish Come in Dancing

the fish come in dancing
iridescent
dark torpedoes
flurry of white silver
spray
as they jump

pulling lines Len says
Christ they're strong
big silver muscle
running from the boat

nylon brands
deep
cuts on your fingers

cicatrices

your blood mixes
with theirs

the fish come in dancing
fifty coho heavy
in the fishbox
off Sangster
and the gas running low

clean them to the scream
of seagulls
blood & guts crawls
into every crack

you throw them up
at Norpac & god
they flop flat and
dull rainbows on their sides
fade

it gets harder to love
the things
you kill.

The Road Taken

Every dawn a new start
yesterday you turned
starboard out of French Creek

no one was talking

hold your coffee cold
watching the others
toss up good catches
you guess you missed
a big school at Bowser

this morning you're mad
get out before dawn slits
the sky pink
run a bit

watch your white pigs
disappear
behind you into the murk

and suddenly the bells are
ting ting tinging
tag lines stabbing like
accusing fingers down
into the sea

first out and all these fish

someone calls but you
don't answer
curse the pigs for
coming in so slow and
one damn coho even hits
a P1A hanging behind
fouls all your gear
but marvellous splashing coho
on damn near every line   flip
the kicking fish into the box
got no time for coffee but
with a last bang and ring
they quit

every morning the same
ending.

Fog

Fog:

　　　you dream

white blind

　　　nothing

solid out there

gurdies good
hard clanking brass

　　　you dream

dark shapes

　　　nothing

you could

　　　walk

　　　into this

　　　soft:

　　　silence

you fish in nothing
words can thumb
　　　　　or
　　　finger.

Deadhead

it is what you
cannot see
the drowned log
swimming dark under
water
like some Grendel
torn from earth and
unforgiving

it is what you
cannot hear waiting
to beat its dumb
point up like a great
fist through
gumwood planks

it is what is unspoken
of boats gone
without a trace
as if some great bird
lifted them dripping
from the sea

it is like
walking in thick grass
in snake country
watching 20 feet ahead
for the thing to rear up
and strike

against wind & water
skill & guts
against this

is what you see
in the faces of fishermen
squatting on the dock.

from

NANOOSE BAY SUITE

I dig the bones softly
femur orange with 300 years
of settling restless in its bed

small bones the backhoe sniffed out
with its blind snout.

What can I imagine of this dominion
this province of lost breath?

a sixteen-year-old girl in 1683
in this dark gravel
her flesh ravished, her dark lover
death coiled heavily about her.

How many times has this earth been
dug how many times love's
dancing feet splayed for the centuries'
discovery?
strange curl of the hips
twist of the back

a half-round dirt lead ball
rattles out of the ribs
onto the trowel

violence her brother   the act
mindless   against the hips
fists   the shot

the hasty dirt thrown over

some white man walking
back to his tall ship
a Haida warrior head high
exulting his kill

softly about the light bones
I trowel for the full
shape of death

and I am lost in this
dark shadow.

⌀

Always by ellipse
love grains and circles
the fractal shape
of time
the simple factor

*That we are all star stuff
woven in space*

These words even now resound
out of the silence
reflect the light of random
collisions in the energy
of the brain
burst into breath

*that we are all
imagined*

writhing from mouths of two
headed dust snakes
we are cast
from debris worried
up   breathtaking

leap of fish into air

dinosaurs' thighs slow
in congealing ice

upright on the earth at last
about this bright bay we dance
for our stars

our beginnings and end
sung in the ever coiling
light.

    ∞

How the word must be put upon
each thing we do not
know   to hold us tight/in space.
the Bay itself a cacophony
of understood sounds/gulls/sea lions/
waves and wind
named

Sno'no'Huas   to push in
written only as each white man
puts the sound in ink on paper
Sno'no'uas
Snonoos
Nuas
Nanooa
Snaw-naw-as
The Spanish Galiano sailed past in
Canal de Nuestra Signora del Rosario
George Vancouver missed the entrance
Captain Richards in HMS *Plumper*
bound the Bay to a Queen and her dictionary
wrote in the ship's log, 1859
entered & mapped this day of our Lord
May 15, a fine harbour 21 miles N.W.
of Nanaimo, with 16 fathoms deep
water anchorage called
Nanoose Bay.

It is the shape of fall

sunlight on Nanoose Flats
gilds the hair of a girl
and four horses bright-flanked
standing like a wheel of flesh
in the October sun

sumac trees   a burst
of blood
cantata from the heart

four curled fingers
of a red maple leaf closing
like a clenched fist

that this is not loss

only that light
shapes us to its
spectrum

this season
stirred
palette green into yellow/red
brown mud swirl
at the end and white

snow
from which the shape
again shoots forth green
crocus tips of
understanding

random

like the body chosen
in the great salmon run
of sperm

blind act or

love   it does not
matter

as the horses circle
the young girl
brilliant
in the centre of the field.

∞

As the herring burn bronze
silver   flash
how it is all one *flesh*
how we all derive blood thoughts

consuming is growth, is instinctive
move up & out

aware also

the Styx becomes that stretch of water/tide
we row against
to the rock island
of sea lions, the great blubbering mass
breeds raucous

downwind the sea lion's breath
the pure herring rot of death

mouthing blabber at night
roll & splash under the winter moon

death gambolling under the stars

that for all of us this is the season
drawn together by our need
by the growth

simultaneously
the sea claims us.

∞

In snow light as candy floss
the seiners diesel in

seen from the air   a million herring
pulse like a blue
bronze python writhing
on the edge of the sand

milt   a sacramental white cloud
stains the Bay

the boys are here for the gold rush
round-up/hold-up of that roe
100 grand each pull of their great
nets bulging with fat-bellied
herring

in Japan a spoonful costs
a bottle of Chivas Regal

all night seiners hammer in
for the opening
anchor in the Bay
by the dozens
wait for the whistle to let fly
roar a circle with their nets
about this solid flesh of herring under
& around them so thick they say that
even Pete the Apostle could walk on water
in this Bay

And at night they are a city
based on the exploitation of this flesh
the Bay becomes a certainty of lights
strobe & cabin & port red & starboard green

dancing in the dark
at this begetting.

    ∞

I spit into the wind but
underneath my feet   in the scrabble
of rocks sucked back   a small hole
like decay or truth opens to
the sea's tongue

that we are all the sea's

one day the sea will take
all this land/house/garden/books
and its pretension

back to a grim salt heart.

The boys out early
shovels & buckets at the August
sand

by noon   five feet high
palisades   walls   moat
a tower on every corner
for each of them to stand
and shriek contempt
at the rising tide

by four p.m. it surrounds
dissolves this fantasy

one by one the walls
fall
each tower in turn
melts underfoot

and they splash   laugh   plan
an even bigger effort
tomorrow

as if the sea's jurisdiction
is only equal to their
skill
the will to build
rebuild
the constancy of image

that this, too, must sing
beyond sand
moat and walls
that time may ebb & flush
about interstices

strength, too, its keep

the strung harmony
of will.

∞

Last night thunder thick as dark
honey
spikes lightning
fire flowers in the woods
about Mt. Arrowsmith.

Out of the smoke at dawn the great Mars
waterbomber repeats/like Sinekwa/ the beat
blunt beaked, swoops the Bay
at first   a trickle of exhaust between
the mountain   four engines bumbling
louder   the huge plane levels out
for its water run.

A mile away its wing tip pontoons sway
six feet over the sea   it glides lower
as the bomb bays open in a great slash of spray
sucks up tons of water into its gut
slow and & low over the Bay in a loving rush
it staggers, till its belly full, the throttles pull
wide open.   The spray hisses   the wings
lift like a gut-shot goose, the waterbomber
roars & thrashes at the sea's kiss. Three, four, five,
six hundred yards.   The bomb doors closed.

It will never lift before the breakwater
lumbering inch by inch unwilling into the air
slow as a heron, ungainly as a crow, the plane's
wings and engines flailing, the plane
seems stopped in the air by invisible
claws yet it soars in a slow turn over
Maude Island to return to the fire.

All this is mythology
Thunderbird whose wingbeats are thunder
and the ocean falling from its body/rain
the great bird lifted from the water
to return to the other element
red eye of its feeding
the water falling
like a benediction
onto the bloodied earth

and I wonder who flies this bird
how it feels when the plane jumps
1,000 ft after the release and the
blistered air boils & tosses the huge
Mars like ash

today, all day, swung in and out of the Bay
like a restless lover
this waterbomber flies only for the flames
tomorrow and again, until every fire
is out.

∞

In Korea he flew Sabres
came out of the cumulus near Inchon
got a long burst in at the Red Joker
in his MIG, and miraculously missed

now he trims and double-checks
eyes flicker over the panel   his hand
over the co-pilot's on the throttle
fires a shot of red fire retardant
into the sloshing belly of the bomb bay
guides his four-engined relic
which does not fly so much as slowly
claw its way up over the mountains

take-offs and landings, the two dangers
of flying twenty times a day
his eyes puckered & red with the strain

sometimes they pick up a salmon
in the run across the Bay
silver as air
it tries to swim
mad flap as it drops
to the fire

once they sucked in a seal pup
heard screams and scuffling, even above
the engines   saw the dark struggling
figure wailing/flail
onto the red gout of flames.

∞

The co-pilot is twenty-seven, blonde and scared
of the massive Mars
like a bumble-bee it should never fly
and he is afraid it will drop one trip
into the glowering red mass below
or stunned with water, fail to rise
and dash its bulk into these mountains

sometimes he feels himself lifting it
with his thighs, his penis retracting
after the bomb bays close, but he is most afraid
when the water drops, and the Mars tumbles
flutters like a leaf in the hot
roils of air over the fire

at night he dreams he is the seal pup
falling, and cannot make love to his wife
because that too makes him lose control

he is ashamed that he threw up in the cockpit
when he saw the seal drop
but the skipper simply trimmed
the rate of ascent, throttled back
grinned at his white shaky face.

∞

On this April morning
brant babble and dip
about the break
of the wave on Sunset Beach

rufus-throated
hummingbirds zing blood red
bullet bodies
about blushing
apple trees

submarine! my son calls
submarine!
black hulk snaking half submerged and silent
in to Nanoose Bay
thick bow wave curls the sea
back upon its haunches

I know this is no Eden it
penetrates
a man with say adenoids
and a wife who wants to
move back to Mum in Nova Scotia
a '76 Chevelle and a kid who gets
cavities
guides this thing
my boy names as toy
submarine! he cries
a fairy tale name
delighted as he would be
at an eagle or a bear

locked somewhere between
ignorance and fear
I know
there can be no talk of apples
this year
without this shape
swimming in my mind.

          ∞

A drowned bull in the sea
black deadhead hangs
above the twin forks and bull head
below the water, trunk twisted and hideous
branches into half animal, half
fable

swung between the low and high
tide in the Bay, between thought
and dreams

The moon is full
silvering this ponderous beast
waiting in the ebb of night

Mimir guarding his own wise death
spread under water, Yggdrasil

at the mouth of the Bay.

          ∞

The Bay is going under

oysters shucked by the gallon
clams by the potato sack
kilos of salmon/cod smoked
in Little Chieftain boxes

and who believes the helicopters
womphing by with torpedoes
slung like unruly bears in nets beneath

and nuclear subs sneaking
unofficially in   missiles
loaded for flight?

for when this rich sand is moon
scape this parasitic tent-life
will fold and straggle North
& South

to lights its Colemans like candles
at another sybaritic embrace.

∞

Nanoose Ridge, a black razor
cut against the moon, hung
like a blind white eye
over my left shoulder

stumbling up the deer trail
5 a.m.   stars fade in this grey
seep of dawn

like a sight for the first time
Edenic the Bay grows
out of the dark

the 30-30 barrel is cold
as pain, and I rub my right
hand against my heart, and wait

the first sounds spin up
from the earth
quick pant of bird's wings
unseen, a grouse bursts
and bats in the bush
at my back

and then the first song chords
woven about me in the
undergrowth
an intaglio of bird calls
silver in the dawn

and I am fixed in this substance

as light opens the tree line
and a three-point buck
steps cautious as a blind man
out into the slash
forty yards away

and I lift the rifle but the deer
thrusts his head towards me
nosing the air as the music
warbles about us, and I level
the sights on the buck's head
v and tip

but my sight goes white
and I cannot

burst into this cantata
with a shot, for I am of it
stillness and silent breath
my suited contribution

the buck high-steps
back into the firs

the birds whirr
into silence

I shoulder my rifle
clatter down the slope
to where the first woodsmoke
rises from the houses
a benediction in the cold
air above the Bay.

∞

Flushed free the oyster spat
floats in insecurity

language of its conception
forms only in its random search
for the place

a rock to cling to
discover the soft coherence
of its form

the slow shell gleaned
from tide after tide

the iridescence within
and on that soft palate
like a tongue, white
and dark-veined
the oyster moves within
its strength

as we too seek our place.

They pull the old destroyer out again
relic of the Coral Sea
one tug leading another, nudging the stern
grey ghost in the January snow
as she passes   gun turrets strangely
silver pure

out in Whiskey Gulf she becomes
a green blip on a radar screen
an electronic twist & turn, like a pheasant
hunted out of the woods

here sport and war blur the blood
this old game ship, gutted of engine
guns, and crew, dodges
ghost torpedoes under her shallow draft

and overhead the spotter plane sniffs
circles with its huge radar nose
for the submarine running
in the canyons of the sea
the crew crouched before
lights on a blue screen
and the electronic diversion
of an orchestrated kill.

⚭

At dawn a child
sings me awake

below the front window
a little Indian girl
crouches over pebbles
tosses & catches the spinning
shards

nor do I know
the song she chants
in quiet sea light

and by the time I am down
the stairs
and to the front door

she is gone

only the mound of stones
like a cairn

reminds me
of other

bones.

∽

Like a lover
the frost makes its patterns
only in the dark

at dawn I crunch out to the shore, sea
heavy as sump oil
underfoot, the artistry of cold
cracks
fern leaves laid out like medieval
maidens white and star-crossed

how is it that these fingers
fashion such filigrees in the grass
eyes of Artemis sparkling
in the soft light

I pick up a feather of ice
forged on some ice anvil
over the bleak earth
over the bones

even as I hold it like a lover
the edges melt
I close my hand about it
feel the cold beauty
dissolve against the beating heart

I open my hand
all this imagining lost
to water without shape
       like tears.

from

RED CENTRE
JOURNAL

No highway, these rough
grader ridges parallel
solferino sand

we follow, driving automatic
Euclid, a '74 Valiant
of circles, squares, triangles
of imagined steel
dumb to understand
this irritant red sand

here we butt against another
dimension

how to imagine North?

the track we leave
declares no entry or passage
disappears despite our desire
to stake a claim, at least annotate
unsung under or above this earth.

∞

*"You should begin
where it all began —
with the Harbour."*

But what are the entrances?
the Harbour Bridge
broods like a resting swan
dissolves into red tile roofs
bushland scattered
limp as old lettuce

And whose history is this? What began?
where past blackmails the present
swims in its breeding jaws?
there are no convicts in my lineage
nor do I step the time
like a drum for

lashes spaced on a convict's back
gallowsfall
Pinchgut or the moment
of intense light
between water drops on an old lag's
forehead

this understanding is not
a line, more, it curves back
to meet itself
for the Bridge, photographed
through the crystal ball of time
and light
is broken, joins nothing.

∞

Always there is North
the word frontier

pulling in like a camera lens
mouthing unknown
vowels

garrisoned, the city too
imagines only itself

for home the hunted heart
betrays
to brown thigh hills
magpie warble of sky

easy to come a cropper
in this land blown
by its fly and uniform
heritage though the eyes
civilize, and voices
toss back at the shore
join old flesh with new

the frontier circles
backtracks us blind.

၏

This is the journey to make sounds
intelligible
armwrestling North
grass loses its grip
sand runs between
loosening roots

no water

ropes the land about
only a rock or ridge
eases the pain
of unnamed places

for the names the first
white men gave these places
Mt. Hopeless, Mt. Despair

fade into an old perspective
the only shapes
dust camels
billowing
behind the car.

Colour, yes, the mallee stump
ugly as Medusa's head
shivering
I smash against the copper
rocks in cold dawn light
and it splits
like a crusted oyster shell

reveals the red and tan
colours of thirst
agony of dehydration
twisted into flesh
parched yellow gold

beautiful as any pearl
this tight-lipped
sculpture of survival.

∞

Always the flesh
retreats

near Copper Hills
a wedgetail muses
pulling a long red worm

of entrails from the belly
of a big Red
splayed at the track's edge.

Seek the shape
only broken knuckles remain
Olgas, Ayers Rock
The old names
glistening on the ochrous plain
half to be dreamed
in air
half to be conceived
massive and beaten
Ancestors
buried
under the copper sand.

∞

That alone, light owns colour, that size
is the eye's equation of distance and fear driven
flat over red desert to witness, mushrooming, the
      great rock
pulse higher, and as we approach, the colour is
      our movement
under clouds purple revelation moves to orange
as the heavens open, close, light brushes life
into the striated lump, and almost it moves
identifies, almost the eye conceives, guesses
it might be something we know, not dead stone
but a sleeping beast, giant worm, sad sprawl
of man, behemoth, but always Uluru avoids
      that
and the light passes, the shapes merge, the run
of sly creases in its skin diminish, it reverts
to its odd rise and off-centre fall, smooth, it waits
for colour and distance to intrigue the eye again.

In the second place
it is a point
to which we move
which moves from us

roots
like a blind man's feet
shuffle and kick
for water
shape a place by touch
and senses past
named white in desperation
Elliot, Newcastle Waters
against the blank
and blindfold
stagger of the present.

      ∞

Pursue the roots
they tangle into hair
gummed dry with blood

Attack Creek and parrots
like shovel blade spears
writhe in green light

here, the black line held
spears against guns
and Stuart afraid
of what the scorched land held
turned his camels back
to Adelaide

listen, the bones rotate
and whisper *this stand
defended also
the known.*

In the third place
battles by riverbanks
colour of men
extinguished in blood
and cries
explorers and explored
bone brothers
under the sand

at shovel's edge
words mumble
into stone plaques
gums grow out
of split skulls

silent
we rest in their shade

boughs peels in the sun

the journey continues.

∞

In the final place
it is a space
we desire
cut pegs for
ride round in a day
camp by a waterhole
claim it by living there
without question

admire the theft
release the crims
to beaten ploughshares
stock exchanges
pen the sheep
rubberband the bulls
dig our way in, resolve to hold

after, there is a ritual sale
an exchange of paper
something lost for nothing
gained
both sides agree
eager to sign it
get it
in their name

out of everybody's grasp.

∞

Consider the paper then
not worth the signing
mapped but not known

circled by feathered shoes
we are always lost here
belonging
only what we say
we belong
to

will not be held
land always within
crying to get out
Kookaburra absolute
parodying itself in glee

while we stammer for the vowels
crying
cry to get in.

∞

Journal entry May 5, 1987: Two hundred miles later, he thinks
he finds his grandfather's ex-land, takes his waterbag, kicks
paddy-melons aside, walks up over two red sandhills. On a rise
he finds three broken walls, remains of a stone house, and
nearby, a circle of stones, maybe mystical, more probably an
old windmill stand. He turns in a circle. Everywhere the red
ribbed sand undulates from his feet away to a purple horizon.
He is lost in the silence.

He sits as flies buzz about, remembers a publisher's
party in Montreal in the late 70s. Fat white flies of snow slap
on the window. He meets an Aboriginal poet, Kath Walker she
called herself then . . . now Odgeroo . . . her dark eyes move
over his face, he's self-conscious, she asks him what the hell
he's doing in the snow in Canada, why he's not in Australia
writing. He doesn't have a decent answer. She touches his
hand with long black fingers, fixes his gaze, says go home,
the country will sing you.

He retraces his steps back to the road. Halfway, stops.
Stares in disbelief. There at the side of his tracks, one
footprint. Barefoot, almost covered in drift, barely discernible,
the stubs of toes dusted with fine red sand. One footprint.
Bisecting his tracks. One strange barefoot track, half covered,
by itself in the lone and level red sand.

Driving down the track
I follow a white tunnel
even the hawks, once hunters
now survive on side-swiped
carrion, shiver and boomerang
about the straight ribbon of bitumen
waiting for the caravans and buses
and road trains to kill for them

like this steer, eyeless
skewed on a bridge
over a dry dust creek
stink and flies and paper
dry hide — and the hawks
fly up only at the last
second as I
white-eyed and fixed dead ahead
roar right past.

       ∞

How to unlearn the single
land of vision, break out
across the waves of orange sandhills
set across our sight.

       ∞

It is the colour black
we have pushed from our palette
which dances back
Banquo in holograph

tjuringa stones kicked aside
for station markers
like stakes in the heart
of this red lore flowing
like sand but surer
than water in this land.

And on the flag pole at Uluru
above the cornered Union Jack
and Southern Cross, higher than
the diagonal Eureka stars,
the black rectangle above the red
centred by the yellow globe.

⚭

I do not climb the rock
vertical trench dug by unnumbered
tourists' feet, clinging to the staked
chain as if conquest is knowledge

rather, I walk about its base
east to west, but first
superstitious perhaps, so something
can smell me, like putting your hand
down to a growling dog's nose
I shove my hands
under my armpits
to get my scent, place
both hands palm down
on the shiny red scale
of Uluru, say hello
my country, this is me,
can you sing me straight?
Or have I come out
of this earth, white, without
the land dancing within?

Thirty thousand tourists each year
dawn snapshot of Uluru, half
an hour of the Olgas and off
to climb the rock like Everest
toil up, hand over hand
on the chain, the need
to conquer it stronger
than any need to reflect

and up they go and top it
a single file white line
winds European
and red sand blind

and below, fenced off
the sacred sites, useless now
because a mob of video buffs
would throng to gawk
at the enigma of black initiation
necessarily secret, the scars
on face and chest, blood
stopped with ash, the secret
wound of knowledge, thrashed
into triviality by tourist thongs

and so the rituals fade
like beautiful flowers, lacking
the husbandry, the fervour of faith, the hands to carry
out the act, the tone to sing
as they were sung,
unworthy, uninitiated, the young
cut loose from the land
wander in a grey world
not white, not black, not
understood,
their tjuringas lost, stolen,
traded for booze,

these sites
doomed to the silence
of our ignorance and time.

∞

The night before I leave Uluru
I build a campfire, dry gum
spurts into flame, the spiders
scatter like my convictions,
disappear, as the flames suck
and lick reluctantly
at the boughs, run
tiny red fingers up and down
as if fingering a flute

and I spread my hands
safe at this distance
to the ebullient flames,
tips resonating in the dark
iconoclastic melody
I feel
their controlled but becoming
warmth.

from

COBALT 3

After John Donne

Every man is an island
and each woman too

single and slippery
as conception, grains
as separate as thumbprints
or the unique voice
prints here on the page

Oh, don't bother to tell me
I'm richer not alone
for all the birds of a feather
solidarity is not sung in one voice

and though the eroding sea
has its wicked way with promontories
washing them slice by slice into its will
which diminisheth not

a single dove flew the flood
to a single island of peace

and every song cries against the grain
tossed in the crevice of time

for the sea flushes us to islands
the absolute and bloody best way
it can.

Journey

One day the sun simply
drops

behind my feet the dark cliff crumbles
but I scramble up higher
grab a quick look
at a land I have never believed in
before

one shaving of light
far, far away, flickers
bright yellow
in the monstrous dark

about me
a forest of writhing trees
aphoristic flowers
unspeakable weeds

in front loom mountains
sharp peaks   deep black valleys
rivers of turbulent ebony

beyond a dark snake sea
writhes
under one fragile butterfly
of red gold luminescence
fading as I watch

time is the essence
and in this land there are no
maps

but somewhere I know there is a path
a direction
I must find on my own

I take a deep breath
fix my sight on the yellow light

take the first urgent step

Narrows

We walk by the Narrows
follow some leader or habit or fad
single file on a narrow path by a cliff edge, below
the flood tide, nine knots, whirlpools away
into the dusk

but someone or thing, maybe
you yourself, kicks your heels
you drop
flail in the rapids

you yell for help, go under, yell
again, but no one up there
has a rope or life ring
though rows of them stare,
a few wave, a bunch crouch
for a better view, one or two cry out
as you swirl away.

At first you're frantic
swim madly for the shore
but you're too weak
in the tide rip's
all mindless muscle
you tread water
suck down into a whirlpool
pop up, gasp, spot a man in a white coat
on a nearby rock, holding out a red lifejacket
you grab, whizz by, a bit steadier
but the scrum of tide topples you

you glance desperately downstream
see another white figure
knee deep in a back eddy

he swings out a lasso and you know
you've got one chance to grab it

your hand burns into the rope
but he can't haul you in

and you swing
in the wild water, learn to hang there
for the many hours the tide takes
to run its course.

Phone Calls

The first few times the phone rings
you blow it

No one knows what to say
and you're no help
too angry, scared and bitter
to bother with sentiment, besides
they all seem to have written you
off.

Finally you sense they've all
written it down like a script
they're reading it to you
over the phone, prepared
edited and rehearsed for days

and you realize they're more scared than you
because you a least have felt
the beast grow its serrated tail
within you, but like a leper
you've nearly touched them
with unimagined sores
and their rosy lens has just
dropped a couple of future
f-stops

and suddenly you feel
sorry for them, for their flesh
and their fumbling
attempts at concern

you get a bit stronger
if not wiser, and then the one
call from Australia, so brash
it's real, *"Hey, Blue what's this
I hear about you and the big C?
I'm bloody glad it's you and not me
old mate!"*

And you relax and laugh
at last, at the stupid honest horror
of it all.

Betrayal

No matter what the books tell you
or the full care voices of lovers

you're on your own

cut out from the herd
dropped from the songs and ceremonies
spun off while the green blue
planet turns graciously away

cuckolded by your own flesh

like living with someone
you never suspected before
was secretly a whore
you lie awake at 3 a.m.
with this slut of a body
snoring its gangly bones
of deceit within you

you can't even see
the raucous party in your own
bawdy blood, as the cells gang bang away
dumb glands grinning as they spread
wide, and have it on behind the host's
back, abandoned to the animal moment
while your future and theirs flops
on the screen into a fade, lap and dissolve.

you know the only way out
is family violence
you have to
damn near kill yourself
to clean up their act
open up to radiation
to vomit and shit them out
or poison the mad beast with chemo
in selfish revenge
like some bad Elizabethan play

just to get back respect, yes
just that chance to start again

breathe in the blue bright air
all those about you
walk and talk in without thinking
take so easily
for granted.

Chipmunk

"Look, Mum," little kid in Safeway
all grave sincerity, points at me,
"He looks like Charley Chipmunk"

the mother's hush and blush, she
glances up from the kid

But you've got to laugh
eight pills a day
two bags of green poison a week
a chemo bloat
of a body, a cheek bulge big
as Satchmo on his trumpet

you look like a grotesque refugee from
a Breughel peasant painting

But if only you could find
the golden nuts the Gods
have squirrelled away

crack the shell and eat
the magic acorn of health.

Ferry Ride

Two dolphins at play in the spray
ride the carve of the wave at the bow
of the *Queen of Nanaimo*

how their slick shapes shimmer
in and out of the green bend
of sea
And I am jealous that they know
how to twist force
to their will, bodies easy with power
they roll and turn in the wave

I am traveling to kill cells
strap myself in for a dose
of chemicals glugged into my veins

pumped through my blood

caught in
this wave of destruction
I must ride the curve of pain
surf in the white crest
away from the steel bow

like these dolphins easy
in their flesh
ride the way back
to the calm waters
of Departure Bay.

Shield

She fits you for your shield
tape measure about her neck
mouth pursed like a seamstress
she checks your nakedness
bare to the bone
against an x-ray of kidneys
lungs heart

no bronze dragons, pennants, embossed lions rampant
this shield is lead
curves and squares to fit up into
the cobalt light

and her bright Brit voice again
"Do you have a family coat of arms?"
the cold tape end touches my heart
"No," I say, *"only family jewels
and will you protect them?"*
but she only giggles, says
she's giving me a brand new
shield, one off, uniquely mine

"And now for the hero part," she smiles
*"something special to remember me
forever,"* and she produces a needle
black ink, pricks two tattoos
one low in the groin, one high
on the chest, *"To line you up,"*
she says, *"in the spotlight for the fray."*

Last thing on your mind, the glory
of battle, forget the Greeks and Achilles
brought back splendid on his shield

you're in a back alley fight
with only teeth and nails and boots
and all you want to do
is crawl out of it
alive.

Monster

Blue jeans three sizes too big
hung with fireman's braces
to put out the fire of
irritated skin burnt from chemo
radiation, and Extra OS shirt to keep
any rub of arms, shoulders, back
at bay

your face bloats up
to suit this new inside image
balding redneck, hippy hick
off a Hornby Island farm
Cat hat jammed tight to hide
the falling hair

but the worst is the knot
of poisoned
carotin in your fingernails
that flattens the tips
then curls them up at the edges
so they shatter at the scissor's edge
like glass
grow concave, writhe
at your fingertips

and your toenails spread
crooked as arbutus trunks
brittle as sugar, twist and shout
against your shoes

all this ugly ducking
from the mirror
looking through the glass
at the green grass field
of health.

Cobalt 3

They shuffle him in
shackles clinking
green gown and handcuffs
past the queue of patients
two prison guards, nightsticks
dangling, for even criminals must be burnt
well
and you watch the guards stare
through thick glass at him
shackled and prone
under the sacrificial light

and you, in your bottle-green
hospital gown, green slippers and cap
next

the bald and halt and just damned sick
wait their turn for the sacred glowworm
crouched against a huge mural of crocuses
daffodils, in a green field
somewhere in a country smelling of health.

Ashen-faced, he's helped out
the lead doors,
you willingly
walk in past the nuke sign
lie down, as the squares of light
line up on your tattoos, one
on your chest, one
on your groin, pulled and pushed
you stay still, the young nurses
joke and hustle out the lead
door

All there is now, the freezing overhead buzz
later, vomit and shit
but the nurse says,
"This is mirror art" as she draws
a red dahlia on your bum
giggles, and all you can do
is laugh, but later, the toilet
stuck tight to your shaking
body, you think you might have to
demand handcuffs and shackles, too,
next time.

Interns

Three of them are waiting when I turn up.
The nurse slaps a green gown in my hand.
"I would prefer white," I say, she sniggers
says, *"Green suits your florid complexion."*
"Not to mention," you add, *"my fading red hair?"*
(*what's left of it, sweetie,* she thinks)

"Just get undressed," she says, flat as a used
spatula, whisks the green curtain across

and I enter my island of floating flesh
lie down like a lamb in open green
as the line of interns forms outside

three at a time, not a gang grope this, but
serious medical experience, a hands-on
fingering of non-Hodgkin's fickle rosary of lumps.

The first one can't find anything.
An Asian girl, Coke-bottle glasses
her Mum's told her not to touch
anywhere near there, she jerks
away at first, then I
guide her tiny hand, clear nails, slim fingers
trembling to the string of pearl
lumps in my neck, my belly, my groin
her hand like a wren fluttering in fear
near my cock, *"C'mon,"* I say, *"It won't bite
but you've got to feel under,"* and her
tiny fingers flash in for a furtive
second, and *"No,"* I say, *"not those two,
the tiny ones underneath,"* and she
pulls back, puts her hands behind her back.

The next one's a big hairy jock
tries to push in against my hand
can't feel a thing, and *"Listen, mate,"*
I say, *"it's like making love, the softer*
the touch, the more you'll get in return"
and his paws relax a bit, finally get on
to the puffed up vanity row of cells.

But the third one, a girl with cinnamon eyes
cool hands, has it, instantly, glances at my face
the moment her forefinger touches the first
grape globe, and I nod, and she senses also
the freeway pileup, chain collision, knows the slow
crash of dumb cells, sees in my eyes how
they screech and smash, feels
the brawl in my blood hears
the silent screams in my head.

Ten Green Bottles

The nurses clip by quick and clean
starched white uniforms
order in their trim shapes
practised smiles

They all march with such confident
strides, their roles
important and sharp
as their triangular hats

You sit with a sprawl
of nine other patients
in a row of seats
against a white wall
waiting in green hospital gowns
your slippers unsure, slipping
on the polished linoleum floor

The docs saunter by in twos and threes
white housecoats flaring, ties, jackets
you catch a snippet of a golf game
or the Vegas vacation, or the new BMW

You admire the square of their lives
the cut tight system they control
their ship-shape mathematical pattern
in this maelstrom of disease

the belief so sure in the future
you hear one doc say he's enrolled
his newborn already
in some private British school

you try to understand
how they live by measuring disorder
balancing probabilities of flesh
drip feeding decay
yet seem untouched

you try to bridge the gap
between their flesh and yours
imagine the minute cancer cells
raving in their flesh

they seem impervious
untouchable, as solid as the concrete
wall at your back

but you know
you're just one of the ten
green bottles on the wall
and you hope it's not you
who'll accidentally fall.

Decrapitation

the hot light fades
on clear plastic memory
yellows and cracks
breaks in the sun, blows
into fog   swims in lazy and thick

the curtain falls, the director shouts
cut, that's a wrap
and all the frames coil up
tight in a can, shoved away
on some dusty shelf

you forget

the rat stink fear, muscletight
chest, watery flush in your belly
hair fallen on your pillow
hairless groin, puffed up baby face
the coppery panic taste

you carry your bag of tricks back to work
turn the key in your office door
sit at your desk, as if nothing happened

but outside the landscape has mutated
the sure dark path down   tilts upward
to a weird sunlit hill ahead

and you don't dare look back
for fear that all you've won
will turn to pillars of salt in the fog

But you can still fast rewind
appointments, dates, hospitals
doctors, nurses, attendants, friends
in the film noir you starred in
but never want to see again

and you're surprised
the dromedary world has gone on
in its dull trot of timetables, meetings, deadlines
the impossible marathon in and out
of the endless mundane maze

but the shadow rat sleeps still
in your flesh, wakes some nights
scurries in the tunnels of your bones
and you jolt bolt upright
into a role you know
you never want to play again.

NEW POEMS

The Bones Rotate

The bones rotate
deep under sod they spin
with the stars
Venus and Mars
rise and fall at the moon's whim
singing in the soft soil
of their upright life in air

always as if in bed
they toss and turn
over the aeons aching
for the north south
true magnetic stance

and the soil dances
in eye sockets   pirouettes
through the gap teeth
and tectonic plates trembling
shudder and turn in their sleep
rocking the bones awake

until folded in symmetry
the lost and found and deceived
femur to tibia to clavicle
like pipe organs they resonate
in the hollow wrung bones
a symphony of DNA

sounding and blowing like whales
in the deep earth.

White

At base the colour white
answers to no one

does very well spun
with deft brush
turning any blood red
to pretty pink

splashed on any canvas
white will mute
any dark colour
to anonymous gray or fawn brown

washed over
yellow or green
white may add
to the light turn
of true blue flags
in a clouded sky

and white as light   as bright
as air
magnifies stigmata
fish eyes all cicatrices
and vaselines the lens
of the red cross on white
samite   clothing the chain mail
of every crusade
sailed across any seven seas
white will spill and spread
like milk or salt

promising sugar
and soak unseen
under the grass into the soil

but what white cannot do
is hide its tracks
grey ghost footprints
or white whorls
and deadly filigree
fingerprints
it leaves
on the green and blue
turned orb of earth.

Underpin

Something is under-
pinning it all, a clock
work fluid as sea   tide
or love, moons us

clicks in, oiled to understand
before the claw's grasp, mouth
opens to kiss or bite or laugh

Under the some-thing-pin
a fluid repeater rocks its pendulous
arm, liquid as light or hate

blind but sure-footed
as the goat
man dances woman, pins
under the fluid
breaks, mouth open
the clock breath clicks
in again
and what pins
fall to skill, fall
under the clock-clicked ball

rolling forever in the sky.

She Rises

She   rising creates her own circle
arcs it with her palms
rounds it in symmetry

places it like bayleaves
on her head
draws inside its aching circumference

imagined as a series of circles
she slides down
stairs

into a coil
flung upright she skips it
swinging the thin light
umbilical   over
her head   under her feet
faster   faster   helix emerging
bright as full round moon

she runs inside
lowers the bracelet of light
to her hips
swings it about hoopla
hula

stops   to drop
the circle rattling about at her feet

and at the orbing rise
of the blood-red sun
she steps
out   into the plain
light.

Aussie Rules 1

This ball

pointedly

will not easily
bounce up into your arms
though you run true blue
hard down a dinky di
honest line

always there is the point
against the grain

against the earth
you cannot grasp

for the damn ball rises
gambols abrupt as Fate   throws
you off

off   you stretch out fingertips beseeching   God yes

let it rise up
into your eager
hands

but it drops
kangaroo hops
careers
wobbles sideways

again rises insouciant ever
elliptic
subject only to the flip
of the kip, who knows
two-up, toss
your love up for the big centre bounce

watch the ball fly
like pennies spinning copper bright

bounce   hop skip and jump   fall
where they may

Aussie Rules 2

My father played every kick
centre bounce and boundary throw-in
roved errant balls   flew
for every mark   played on   took
the handball running through
danced the game Dionysian
elbows and hips in the crowd

how he loved the game   hated
the unpredictable point
of the ball   its erratic dip
spurt and jump   knew
somehow it was linked to her
my mother's amazing and pointless
disappearance

jammed next to him the rare time
he was home   on the mound
at Adelaide oval he flinched
every tackle   jostled every ruck
elbowed my ten-year-old ribs as he
dove into the pack
shook his head at the white
blind justice of the ump

but saved his clenched and just anger
for the vagaries of the pointed ball
its capricious twists and turns and careless
bounces   how its whims
beat even the best Bob Hank
Paul Bagshaw   Motley and Deane
how his body urged the ball to behave

contorted to urge the flying punt
up through the tall white posts

and after the siren's wail and defeat
how he stared blind and silent
out the train window at Bowden Croydon
station   reliving the freak bounce
of my mother's death
the inexplicable   twist that   tore
her out of his sure and steady hands

this Grand Final loss
he could never grasp.

Gallipoli: A Gift

She brings it back:
gift in a tiny box
on white cotton wool
one misshapen lead ball
a crescent of rust steel
shrapnel
dug up from the gulley
the Anzacs bayonet-charged
under white hot star bursts
rip   whizz   and tear

still they yelled   ran headlong
into the mad staccato music
of machine guns

young warriors from unlikely places
at a new Troy
not for the King's Shilling
but for pride in the cities/towns
they came from

Melbourne and Cabramatta
Adelaide   Coolangatta
Sydney   Oodnadatta
Perth and   Paramatta

and history rolls heavy in my hand
echoes of Anzac voices
blind young courage buried
turning in this ancient battle earth
with shards of shrapnel
arrow heads   rusted bayonets
broken swords

cannot be held in the molten
cast of frozen bronze
or its wild flight caught
on a plinth in Canberra

gift of blood/love
hidden in deep
billabong silence
rising once a year to wail
its magical siren song.

Chloebia Gouldiae / Gouldian Finch

"Glory be for dappled things"
In all his minute glory
in his limited cage
my male gouldian finch
lifts his head   and sings

so quiet the earth stills to hear
tiny treble from the black throat
ivory beak, green neck, blood-red
head arched, purple chest puffed
golden belly, sea-green back

and he dances on the perch
before the female's critical eye
her black head   lilac chest
thrust in to appraise
the ancient proposition notes

only 2,500 left in the wild
savannah near Katherine, NT
their beauty trapped them in mist nets
rocket nets fired at dawn
over billabongs stacked in Amgoorie
tea chests sold overseas

thousands died in their diaspora
and now they live and breed
on cold Vancouver Island
this 8 x 8 x 6 refugee camp
is all they know

let free or escaped
they would die in a day

yet vestigial, instinctively
they will breed here
only on Aussie time
after the September monsoons
their young grey-green fledglings
easily camouflaged
even in this space
until adulthood draws
them to the danger
of their vivid colours

the puzzle is
how over the ages emerged
Darwinian or not
the astounding explosion of colour
blood red or satin black heads   green necks
black throats   yellow bellies
purple chest   emerald back
startling against the olive land
how this rainbow burst in a tiny finch
came to flaunt itself   offer beauty
so rare   uncommon   desired

to render its own wild
destruction

Mount Baker: Deserted Church

That this new/old country has relics

a single gravestone by the fallen
back wall, broken nave
no flesh between remains
on this sacred acre, fallen rubble
witnesses the defeat even of
Wesleyan iron chains

the stone fence glistens with mica
fool's gold, delicate coruscations of rose quartz

but sober colours still
giving no rise to un-Christian
pride or vanity

but for
Tom Bonython, his slate headstone
RIP 1874, splattered with gunshot scars

his substance sucked up
into the limbs and leaves
of a great gum, roots bulging
from the soil, annual bark
peeling like dumb commandments
in sheets at its base

And I wonder how does
Old Tom in his heretic theology
transubstantiated, waving
eucalyptic to the sky?

New Australian

In Adelaide in 1960
I thought I wanted to marry
a Presbyterian Linden Park blonde

then this woman — who would not wear
pink twin sets
pearl necklaces
tweed or tartan skirts
bobbed hair or balance
a lamington
on crossed knees nor crook
a decorous little finger
over afternoon tea

dressed instead in passionate
black   purple blood-red
wore eyeshadow   swung
long black hair in a mane
sipped thick Turkish coffee
argued with her hands
brown eyes intense with the image
of hammer-and-sickle justice
and when she danced
music rose in her
like a hot flower

drew me right in

my Tusmore aunt told me
we'd have black babies

her Ikarian father clenched his fists
silent over this Anglo Xenos
at his kitchen table

but the first day it snowed
in Canada after our wedding
we held up our tongues
to the unique
and christening flakes.

Daily Bread

Kaldoonera Hill, South Australia

The trick is not to think
or you'll never finish
sewing endless bags of wheat
open to be plumped full
sewn tight   standing
in clumps on the bright stubble

Jacko drops me off
in the Holden Ute, says
only pansies use the filler can
he grabs a handful of wheat
in his calloused fist   punches it
into the top of the bag, *says now*
sew that bastard tighter
than a bull's arse in Spring

102 Fahrenheit
the sun preens heavy
like a wedgetail on my back

he roars off
but in one hour my hands
raw from ramming
hard wheat grains tight
into rough Hessian bags
fingers cut from the six-inch needle
and sewing twine
my sweat and blood
staining the wheat
I pick up the filler can

luckily drop it
just before Jacko roars up
in the Ford Blitz truck, says, *righto*
lift those bastards up on the truck.
Nah, you don't need the hand claw.

My back cracks with the first bag
I stagger. *Jeez,* says Jacko
you're a bit of a daisy, shrugs
throws his side of bags up
squats, rolls a twirlie,
watches my struggle, says
nah, yr more like a bloody daffodil

I learn the trick to lift
is not in the hand claw
but the roll up the thigh, bend
quick   flip up and grab   to hold
the bag like a dead man

moulded to your shoulder
weight straight
down to your knees

but Jacko says, *hey blossom, the trick*
is not to straight stack
the truck but stack those bastards
like a Gyppo pyramid

And loaded
we take the corrugated road
twenty miles shake and bounce
to Poochera railway siding

Right, bluebell, says Jacko
you unload 'em.
He hands me the keys, says
pick me up at the pub
when you're done.

And I ease the bags off
on to the landing
with dried-blood hands
imagining
the broken crust steam
and smell of a freshly baked loaf
white bread melting gold
with butter
a swirl of pink blood
in every slice.

Sacrament

Witness the drought
dust piles in fence corners
of red dust sheep
earth like bacon
crackled with heat
ironic shimmer of mirage water
copper and rust iron sand
witness roll away   the red land
horizon-tied   barbwired   under
a sky hard as blue stone
lizard-leather tongued

to come to this red land again
cracks like dry veins
writhing down the creeks

hear at last the orchestral clouds
roll grumbling above
witness finally the rain
drift in
soft as fleeces
grey drizzle of paint
on white dry canvas

witness the earth leap up
dance brush-cut spikes
of green paddocks of wheat
flowers wild with colour
gum trees spun green

Herefords bellying out
brown bugs of Merinos
head down
caterpillaring emerald grass
parrots blossom up
in a green red shimmer of praise

witness that here only water
is the sacrament that holds us
binds us to this capricious earth.

Logging Protest

Nan, Thailand

Our mini-van halts
at the outstretched hand
of the policeman
on the Chiang Rai highway

on the right-hand side of the road
squat Thais in black singlets   shorts
chainsaws at their feet

on the other side
lotus blossoms of monks
saffron flowers at the feet
of a dozen teak trees

a sergeant argues
hand on gun and hips
with the old monk
seated under a thick-trunked
teak tree

his smile is a sweet
old peach   he nods
his glasses flash
but he will not move

we wait

I ask what the monk is saying
the policeman shrugs, sighs

they translate for me
the monk's smiling words

no tree, he says, no thing
should die
before its time

Faculty Day

Rajamangula Institute of Technology, Nan

We're being blessed
faculty in a row of chairs on the podium
before six monks chanting incantations

flowers at our feet
a bouquet in our laps
gifts from the students
assembled to watch

the head monk picks up a bamboo swatch
dips water from a silver bowl
slow walks the line of faculty
chants quietly as he flicks one shot
of droplets   a blessing on the head
of each professor
he's a bit bored maybe

until he stops before me
the only farang faculty
even on my chair
I sit a foot taller than any Thai prof
and the old bloke pulls his saffron robe tight
smiles an apple-dry smile
chants louder
and the other monks behind him
join in   all sing louder and louder
until   one flick
the water falls on my head

then two
three times he splashes
my face and hair
nods three times as if to say
that was a necessary
farang dispensation
to fill apparent chasms
of Western sin

he nods again
walks on to single bless
one splash
the next Thai prof

A Fish Too Big

At the Huang Goong restaurant
in Nan, Thailand, the fish billows huge
far too big for its tank
on the front desk
by the cash register, the fish
forced to face wide-eyed
every customer, grabs
my Western eyes

Arawanna, three feet of dime-shine scales
in a tank so small
its piggish nose
snubs and rubs on the front glass
its fan tail frays in slow flails
against the rear   too long   it cannot turn
and only its black eyes, silver rimmed
flicker nervously about
its watery jail

on such cruel display
Westerners wish it free

or has it simply grown
too big for its own good

Osteoglissider, big bony water glisten,
it could, in rage or fright
leap out or smash apart
its frail glass prison

but with Thai calm
it undulates ever so slightly
accepts the mirrored space it holds

mai pen rai
the Thais say
or what can you do
about   fate   chance   luck

and what can the fish or I do
about our own shrinking
glass cage of flesh?

Mountains North of Nan

Driving
on a hairpin bend
the Colonel stops the Mazda

we climb out to look up
at the jungle thick above

below us a crater filled now
all lush leaves   rejuvenation
from the B-52 strike in 1966

up there on that ridge
Colonel Poingsat points
they opened up   AK-47s
the jeep windshield shattered
my sergeant hit in the left arm
I pulled him out   got hit myself
we hid behind the back wheels

fired back   M-16s   we went
through two or three clips.

They took off. We
called in an air strike
got the hell out of there.

Later after golf and Singha beer
the Colonel pulls up his shorts
shows an olive-blue scar
on his thigh, looks right at me
says, I was a green lieutenant then
and you, in 1966
protesting the war?
yeah, I say. Looking straight
at him, Yes, I was

he nods, quietly. We sip our beer.
Mai pen rai, he says, very softly.

Image

On Bangkok tv, the global market closes
its cozening fist, subtle as hell
promoting Thai kids with European faces
sipping Coca Cola
and tall Anglo Thai executives
thrusting Budweiser cans at the lens
and even the small Thai girls grow
tall and slim their nut-brown deer
eyes turn Eurasian blue for all
the female magic potions
Chanel and Klein and Versace
blonde skin creams and porcelain
skin lotions, the soft soap club
hammers every night

But even north in rural Nan
I am cut to some quick
when the young woman caddy
on Nan Gold Course touches my white
arm with her slim brown fingers, rubs
her own silk dark skin, and says
I too dark, I want good
white skin like you.

Farang

First weeks in small town Nan
the only farang for miles
you shrink inside, downsize
to fit the demure Thai figure
the lotus hand *wai*
the shy Thai smile
the quickstep walk, the polite deference

you start to think Thai size

with you as Gulliver, the biggest
body in town, ducking under
every awning on the sidewalk
finding no shirts big enough to fit
your gargantuan shoulders
or thongs sufficient
for your enormous farang feet
and apologizing for eating
two Thai meals at one sitting

and the tiny girls
whisper about your hairy size
giggle quietly, so you're told
speculating on your other lower
measurements

but in big city Chiang Mai
on holiday, tourists like locusts
swarming the night market
you feel like Gulliver
back in England from Lilliput
revolted by loud tall Germans
strapping Swiss, outrageous Aussies
giant Pommies tramping awkward
huge and hairy down Taepae Street
their bear-like shamble
broad cattle swing of their rude hips
the dangling rough-haired arms

And you wonder if you dare
face the mirror ever again.

Thai Dogs

In Nan the first time at high noon
I walk the town streets
stumble on concrete blocks sunk at odd angles
the dogs wake up   sniff   sniff
snarl and rush out of the dark shops
into the mad noon sun
a snap pack of mange and leg sores
tails curved tight   hackles stark
noses wrinkled in distaste over bare fangs

I learn my lesson   lose my Ban deodorant
toss out my English Leather soap
eat every morning the Thai breakfast
rice porridge with shrimp and fish sauce

and one week later pick my path downtown
over the same broken sidewalk
past the dogs sprawled in the shade
watch their dozy noses lift to sniff   sniff
find no farang stink
and fall
back into their Thai dog dreams.

McCormack Hospital, Chiang Mai

Steely spectacles on a bronze bust
of Dr. Court in the foyer
founder of the hospital

the farang who trekked in alone
pack mules through the trackless jungle
carrying medicine for lepers, beri beri, malaria
to heal the lame and halt and afflicted
in the trackless mountains of the North
cold burn of Christian zeal
in his pharmacy boxes

in 1948 when I was singing
sunday school hymns for missionaries
in the cold Croydon Methodist Church
the pennies dropping for Jesus
and the poor of foreign lands

Court's vision   the inner steel
of Christian love   as he stumbled
in the monsoon mud to a peasant shack
to deliver a baby   his hands extricating
love from the womb

and the pennies dropped
and Jesus acquired the Karen and Luan and Hwan
hill tribes   but I need to note

the incredible   the driven love
that led Court to the wilderness
to test his faith   deny his flesh
build the healing sanctuary
employ his clever hands
in their Wesleyan zeal to heal.

Monsoon: Nan, Thailand

We wait so long for it
the melodrama monsoon rain

under our feet   tense
heat rises from the coiled earth
we watch the thick clouds roll
capriciously by
air   electric   cobra   coiled

strange that Canadian west coast
rain is more straight up
polite   a small kettle drum
beating constantly
a soft catspaw misting all

but the monsoon here
is a gored ox
bellow and deluge
heavy heave above
splatter up wild from the ground

for three days now   the sullen brows
dark pudding clouds frown
hang upon us
close clothing   we sweat in
glance up at the black roil
slow swirling above

see only the fat clouds roll imperiously by

then at five on a Friday
a series of slaps
left jabs of rain splotches
a dozen heavy wet towels
flop heavily on the roof
ten minutes of roaring
like a jet engine slammed into reverse

rain sloshes down
brick pink soil turns to liquid
red mud and above
the bumble and batter
of thunder clouds

like NFL tackles
grunting deep in their chests
as they grapple and fight

silver flick of lightning
a belly spurt of thunder
not from sky but up it seems
from the trembling earth

downpour blots the view

but again and again the mad
drummer in the sky   lifts
the huge drumstick
pound-beats   one   two   three
massive blows on the grey
elephant skin clouds

the house shivers   air cools

a rattle and roll
like an F-18 diving through
the sound barrier
scatter of white jags
above   all about
a sluice
of water shinnies off the roof
overflows gutters   scoots
down drainpipes   turns earth
into red mud

one lone Honda scooter
putters down the road
driver vainly holding
a billowing red   green
umbrella up   forward
of the handlebars

tomorrow the Nan River will bloat
up like a brown python
swell out over the valley

Thais in their rice paddies
oxen plowing ahead
farmers following
knee deep in the rich mud
bent over under conical straw hats

rhythmically swaying
to sow the green rice plants
in long   water-filled rows.

Aloha

At least she leaves
a goodbye kiss

pink lipstick imprint
floating flat
on a kleenex
in the toilet bowl

Friday Speaks

No, it was never Crusoe's bullying
or the feet kissing   dancing attendance
head bowed   spread obeisance
he craved   an easy gift
for all these bound
him to me   tight as his ego
to the island of his fear

sure, I was glad to be rescued
move from captive to captor
chains he never recognized

for what he thought he built
cabin   crops   goatskin tunic
a spatter of words
I could control
by the mere shake of the head
nod   open hands   a sad look

body language he fell for
with all that white
whirl   hiss   and surf of thought
surging over the coral atoll
his mind built about his flesh

at first he preened
thought he'd saved me
raised me to his exalted state

Man
Friday is a joke, really
we pretended together to shutter off
the taste of mana
the rich tang of blood he'd forgotten
adrenalin rush of the war chase

and hypocrites   we played
handshake friends

I was released from real names
ropes of words   all
those island of obligation
he never did discover
how I freed myself.

Procrustean Bed

In this bed she shapes and scents
the man she brings must never know
the procrustean power of her love

how, late in the smooth slept dark
she will arise and crank the bed's
imagined shape to her best conceit
tape the outsize form, the arrogant legs
overhang, the violent hands
how she will cut with fastidious
care, these outrageous limbs to her size

her hands fluttering like white doves
she will sew
the trembling arteries and veins
sing into his blood her cicatrice
embroider invisible on his skin her secret
sign, the emblem of her love
so other women
coming close to him will recognize
her claim

how he will know nothing of this
awake to her soft curves at his back
hear in her bed, her birds
sing in the dawn
and consider himself
blessed among men.

The Chair

I have put down my tools, hung
the plane, square, saw up
in their allotted space because
the fir, though kiln dry, bucked
its grainy twist, refused me, pulled
its mulish dance against its imagined
shape, resists the straight back, solid
four legs

I hang my apron, hammer down, smell
the sweet chips, shavings fallen
in a scuff on the floor

finally the effort wearies, the wrist
weakens, the eye fails at the straight
run of every edge

I consider that the wood
should have stayed ringing in the trunk
sprung diurnal out to branches, leaves
silent but graceful, its own artisan
with pretense

And I want the simple ground
under its shade, to sit quietly
without the turbulence of process
chain saw to log truck to mill to planer
to the sober struggle of reshaping
to a rump

I shut the workshop door, do not turn
out the light
for maybe in the dark
outside
I will dream the other way
of civil shape.

Photo

a photo, sepia browned with age, drops
out of my family copy of *My Brilliant Career*

and there on a fallen white gum, my mother
and father, circa 1930, in tennis whites
her dress hugs ankles, white stockings, white
shoes, a weird round hat with a wide bow

he in a striped blazer, white strides, white
shirt, collar stylishly upturned, handsome
dog (he knows), smiles

her left hand tentative on his hands clasped
about his right knee

neither look at ease, young, serious business
this courting, faces slightly averted; my
brothers and I still a toss-up in my mother's
eyes, this man beside her, who might do
and I ask

to whom does my mother scrawl
apocryphal on the back of the photo?

> what do you think
> of my latest —
>   smile?

Genesis

The man you try to avoid
peers at you through your chromosomes
at your dilemma

you hated listening to him
but if you listen now you can hear
it is your voice he uses

you catch yourself in a movement
a trick of the face/hands   a phrase
you've always detested

you pass on what you can't avoid
indecision fear delay guilt prejudice
you want to go that far?
in the dark?

all the blind puritan suspicion in you
is him laughing now
as your own son shakes his head

the woman you try to find
argues quietly within you
to let it all grow as it will
take the thorns with the scent
and colour

you have never known her
seen through her eyes

you know only the bald bull head
of the stocky man
who bolts the door against chance
turns the key in the gambling box

afraid to let anyone
out of his sight in case
they'd disappear like her

like her and the memory of a soft
but indistinct voice.

Ice

Here is a camera.   Here is a film.
shot one frame a century

Still
no movement.

Hold your breath.

Imagine white
glacial
ice
grinding
down
a mile
thick
river
five miles wide

its slow, ponderous march crushes all rock resistance
a haughty tongue of ice slow rasps each tip of mountain
abrades ridges, pulverises trenches
until all that lies in the melted ice
flooded by salt sea

my breath
so brief in the sun

my voice singing short
in the moon

which pulls unseen

low green islands hung
parallel in the grey tide.

February Rain

Only Douglas firs could love this rain
endless Pineapple Express roaring in
front after front of cloudbursts rolling
in from the Pacific to dump
sheets of water on this outpost island

until we feel awash, the sea
thunders in on one side, lakes
bulging banks behind, we turn
uneasy in our floating houses
creaking roofs, floorboards shift
like the slight roll of a boat

water laps just below our eyes

our only relief are small mad streams
brown froth tearing at their banks
to run this flood out to the sea

we step back from the eroding banks
forced to retreat upstairs

and in our dreams, our beds
lift under the sluice
of tide and risen water table

up to the roof to crush us
in this relentless rush
of rain.

Xmas Tree

Three days after Xmas
she's at the tree, boxing
back the silver bells and balls
our sons' gold angels, birth stars
pinpoint flashing lights

"Don't," I say
"leave it for a day or so"

"No," she says *"we need the light
and the tree is drying out"*
but the skinny fir I see as jubilant
flower, greening the bay window
pinched from under the power lines
bravely bearing a family accumulation
of historical glitz and bits

But she takes the secateurs
cuts the naked boughs
one after the other to burn
in our Orley woodstove, and again
I protest this brutal degradation
this sacrilegious striptease

She says *"Christmas is a male rut"*
I'm in so deep I can't see over the edge

I watch the boughs fall one by one, fizzle
burst into flames in the stove

I carry the bare-boned skinny trunk
outside, cut it with the swede saw
into seven tiny sticks, stack them
for kindling, feel underfoot
the solid male earth
shake like jello.

Orpheus

Lost in the silence
between the notes
that stilled the beasts
within and without

silenced the songbirds

unlucky in love, lost
to snake's fangs, he dared

the dark and brought back to light
love, only to lose, like all men
a woman to a backward glance
mistrusting his own song
the power of fingers on the strings
not the mindless muscle on the oar
the strong wrist-swung sword, no

ventured into real peril
love and speech and the songs
all women long for

look

Orpheus brought it on his own head
this passion that tore him in the end
ecstatic
limb from limb.

Euclid

Dark in my rectangled bed
on my oblong pillow, the storm
bursts outside, rattles the rectangular
windows, shocks me awake   I switch
on the globe of light, see four   square   walls
square ceiling, right-angled parallel mirror
the framed Picasso print

Outside the windows a jagged streak
a belly grunt of thunder, reveals firs
their tossed arms abandoned
to the wind's passion, its voice
screaming under the long rectangle of roof

Downstairs I pick up a round cup
warm milk from a long cube
Ovaltine from a short tube
again a globe of light attempts
to dispel the darkness I have

fooled myself into believing
lives only outside, distant as Darwin
and the random coin toss, dismissing
the love triangle, Euclid, my hairy flesh
and nature's stony sanguine eye

and my hair stands up at a fizzling flare
so close the blaze strobes the square
of my kitchen
with trembling light.

Surfer

for akr

Impertinent
on the lip
the simple surfer hangs
for sea
endlessly called in from ocean
bounds up like great lions, puffs
a mane of swell, huffs a white
row of teeth, curves
to a green sheen of breaker

all hc has to do is choosc
the right one from the run, stroke five
six seven, dig and up
to a crouch, hover, the board cut
in, ride the board

artist on the edge, always
picking the right time
is everything, seeking
a green tunnel curl, to slip
to a fetal crouch, slick and cool
down to birth

choose the wrong wave
and dumped, the green bowl
spins down to a jar of sand
shock and tumble of suffocating
sea, white board, leg chained
whiplashes the spine, but above
the dim light pulls us up, up

And so we all surf, sit in rows
seek the perfect wave, soft
and pliant underfoot to dance us
down, slip-sliding through
the roar of lion waves
to some imagined sandy shore.

ABOUT THE AUTHOR

—

Kevin Roberts came to Canada from Adelaide, South Australia, in 1966. After completing a Masters degree in English at Simon Fraser University he began teaching at Malaspina University College when it opened in 1969. He has a PhD from Griffith University in Queensland and he has studied in England and lived on the island of Ikaria in Greece. For five years he ran a salmon troller in Georgia Straight and on the West Coast of Vancouver Island. He has been a visiting Professor of English at colleges in Nan, Thailand, and Shanghai, China. In 1985 he was Writer-in-Residence at Wattle Park College in Adelaide. He has made several treks in to the Red Centre of Australia. Under the auspices of the Canada Council, he has toured as a writer and reader of his work across the breadth of Canada. He has published eleven books of poetry, two books of short stories – *Flash Harry and the Daughters of Divine Light* and *Picking the Morning Colour* – and a novel, *Tears in a Glass Eye.* Two plays that he has written, *Black Apples* and *Opening Day,* have been professionally produced by Theatre One in Nanaimo and his play about Tommy Douglas, *Dust on the Moon,* was staged in a student production at Malaspina University College. Both his poetry and fiction have been widely anthologized, and two books of poetry, *S'ney'mos* and *Stonefish,* have been produced and broadcast by the CBC. The Australian writer Nigel Krauth has commented that as a poet Kevin Roberts is known for taking the "common man's point of view and showing that humanity is still connected to the turning of the universe."

MEMBER OF SCABRINI GROUP

Québec, Canada

2006